FERRET
COLORING BOOK

CRYSTAL
COLORING BOOKS

ISBN-13: 978-1546534020
ISBN-10: 1546534024

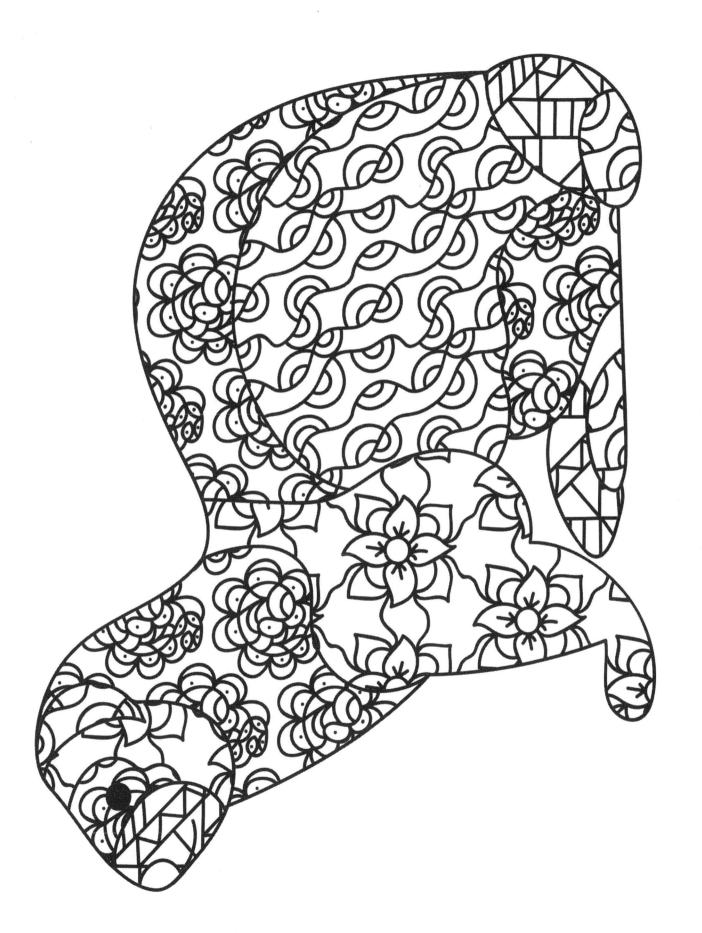

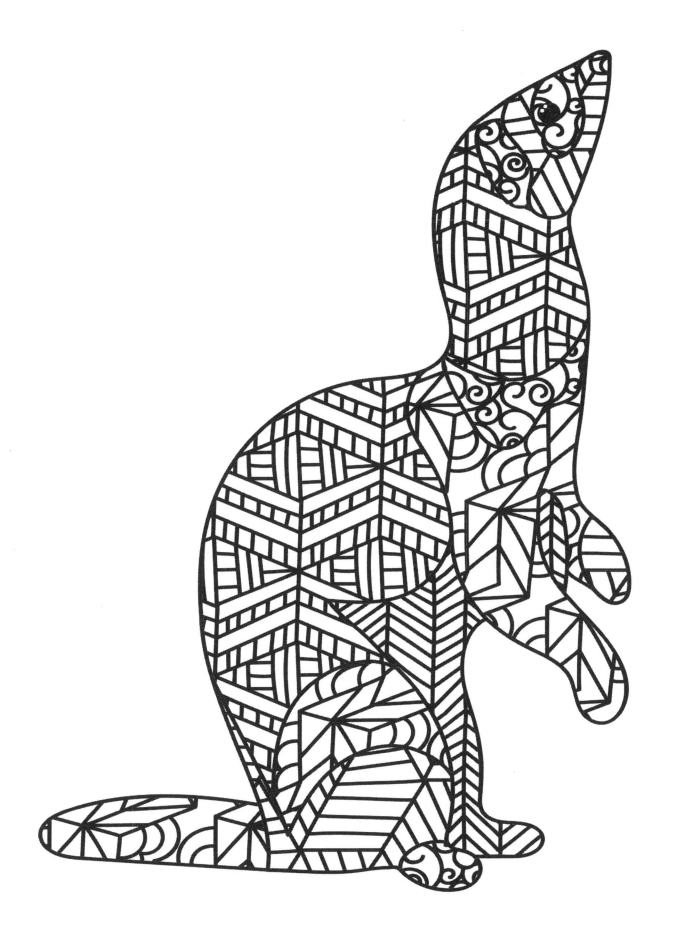

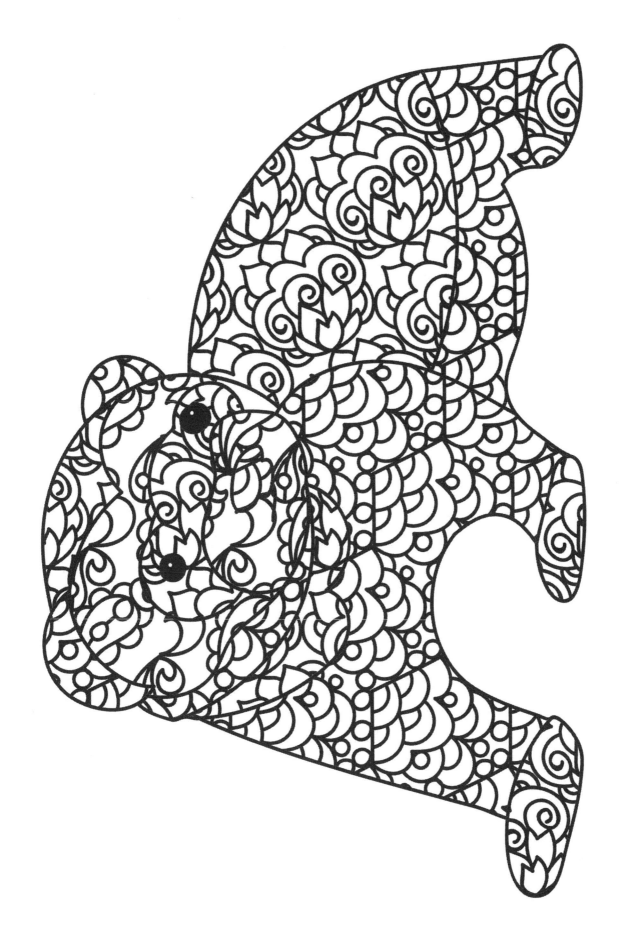

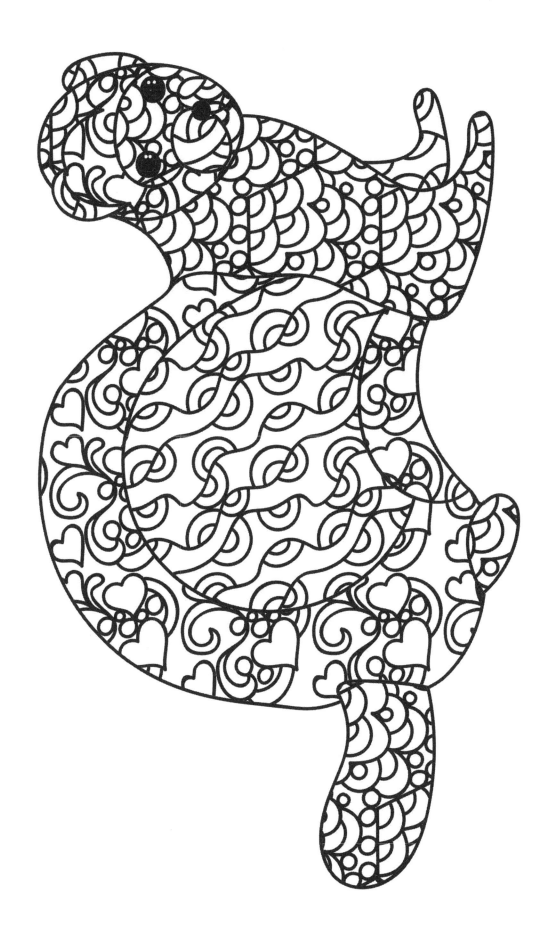

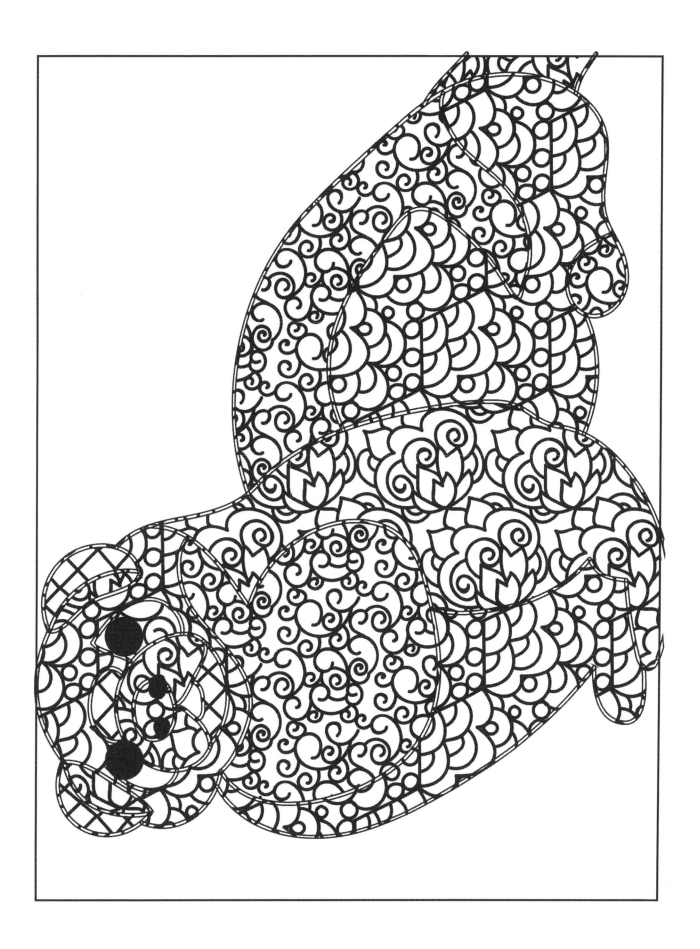

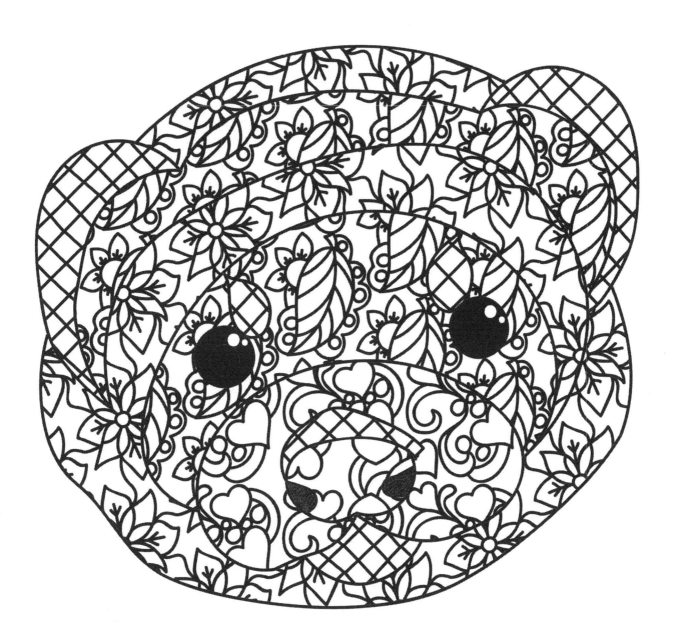

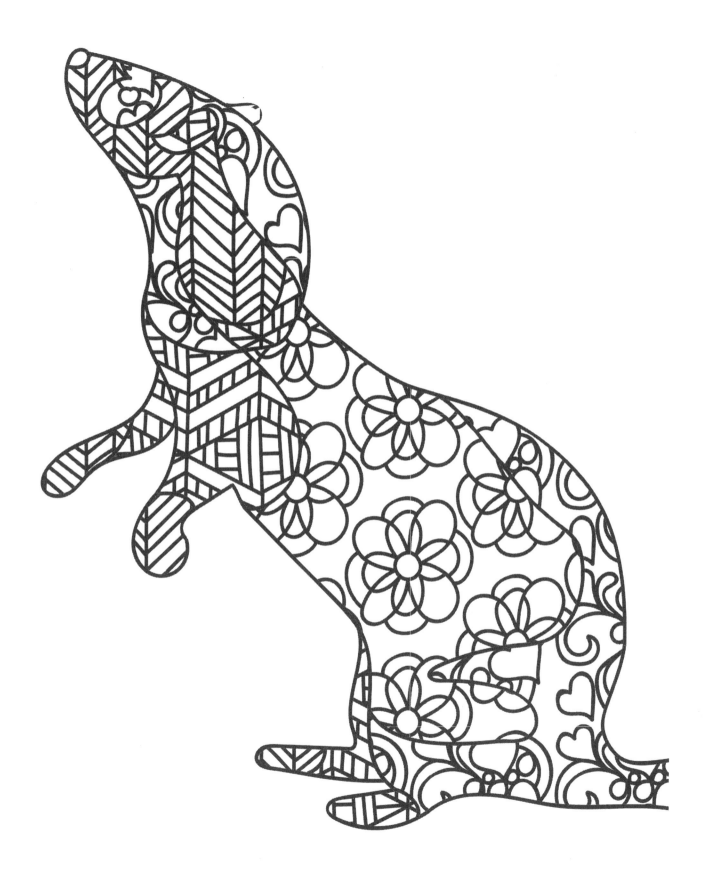

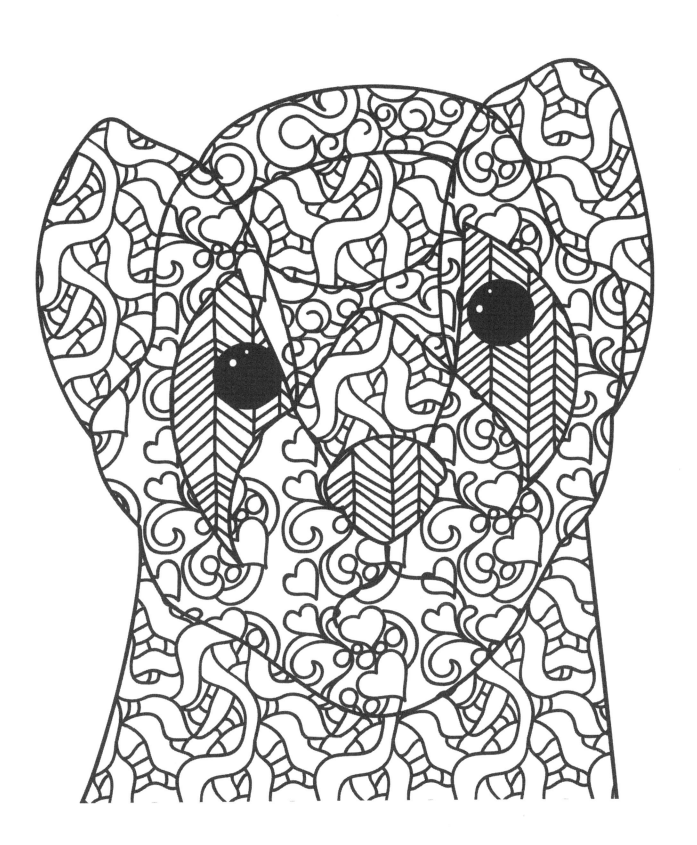

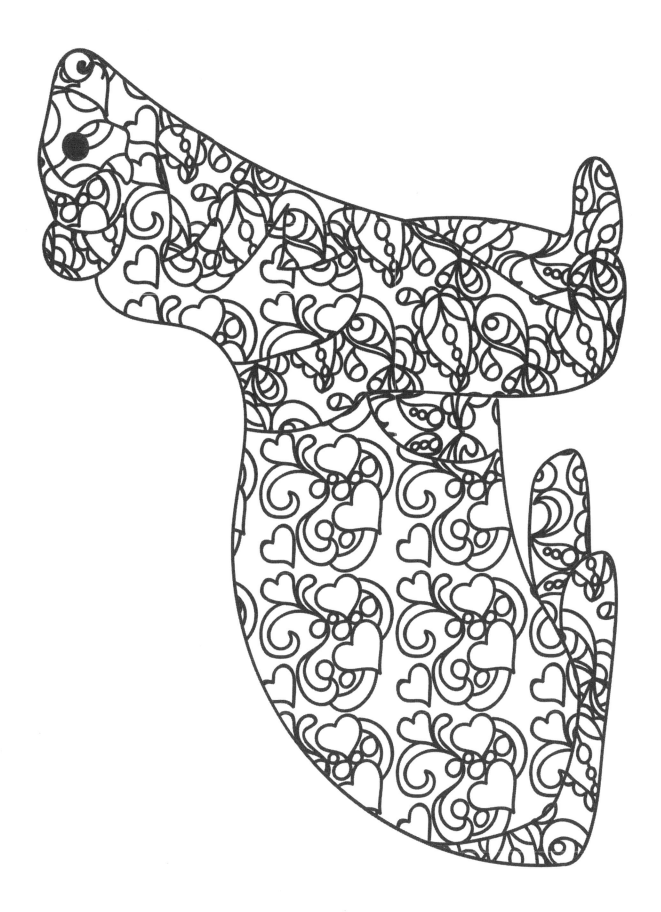

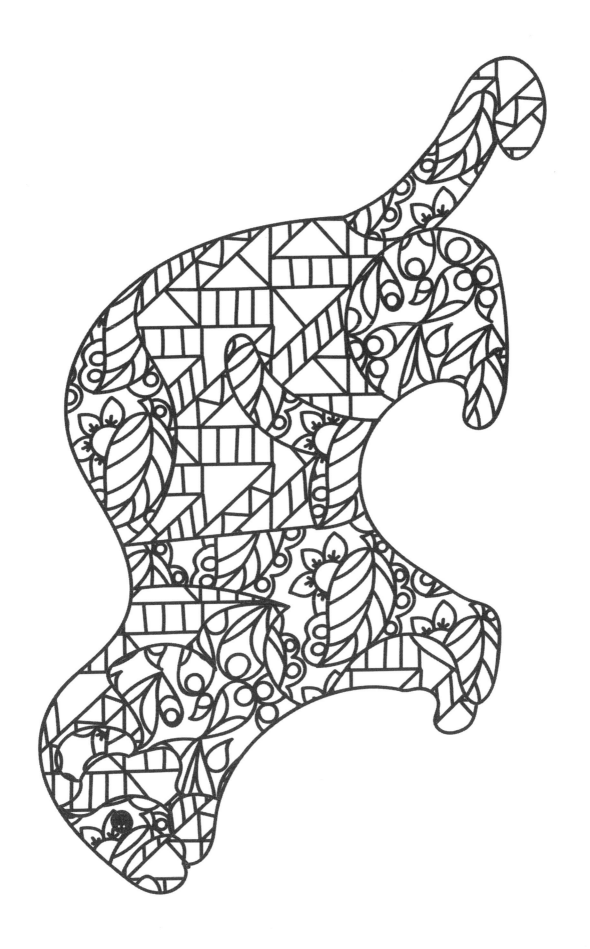

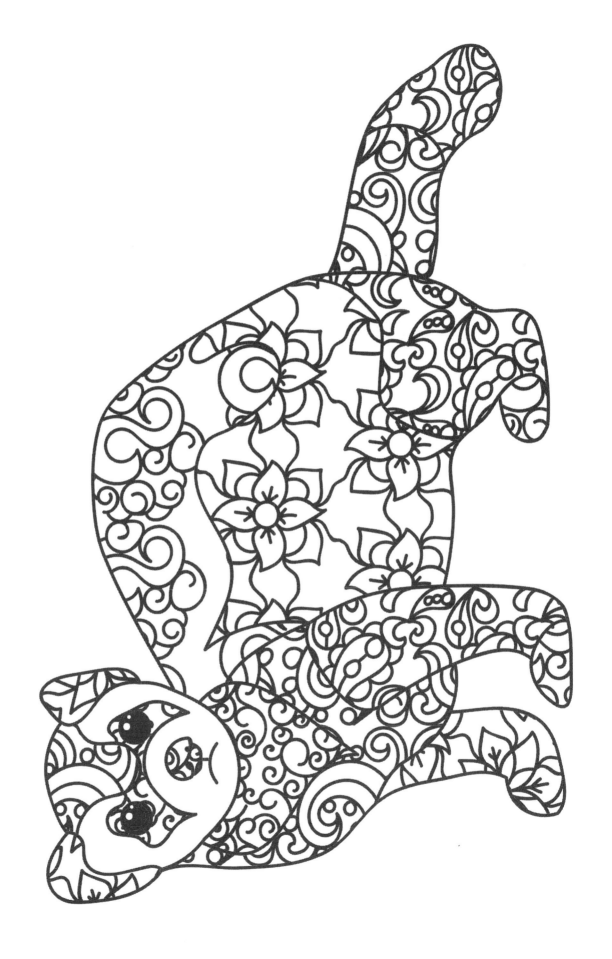

COLOR TEST PAGE

COLOR TEST PAGE

Wario
Nappa
Murdoc
Rwerminger
Waluigi
Zarban
Kakyoin
Mars
Eraken Frog
Shuu Tsukiyomnen

Made in the USA
Lexington, KY
14 December 2018